HARD ROAD TO WISDOM

How vice can pave the way to virtue

CW01496270

Jesal Pankhania

ELEPHANT
EDITIONS

First published in Great Britain in 2024 by Elephant Editions

www.elephanteditions.co

ISBN: 978-1-915921-01-7

British Library Cataloguing in Publication Data. A catalogue record for this book is available from the British Library.

Dedicated to my children, Rohini-Nandini and Vrindavan-Chandra. Be curious, stay hopeful, and serve to the best of your capacity.

Contents

Transliteration and Pronunciation

Sanskrit words have been spelled using the IAST (International Alphabet for Sanskrit Transliteration). This is the Roman script with diacritical marks to allow lossless transliteration. A guide to pronunciation is below:

a	as in sh<u>i</u>rt
ā	as in c<u>ar</u>
ī	as in s<u>ee</u>
ū	as in r<u>oo</u>m
ṛ	as in fathe<u>r</u> said in an American accent
k	as in s<u>k</u>y
c	as in su<u>ch</u>
ṇ	as in e<u>n</u>trap
t, d	as in the Spanish <u>todo</u>
p	s<u>p</u>y
ś	<u>sh</u>irt
ṣ	as the 'sh' sound in the German ge<u>s</u>talt

Foreword

Go into a jewellery shop and ask for the most expensive ring. They'll proudly present it to you, set within a stunning box and inlaid with velvet cushion. More specifically, a dark velvet cushion... dark blue, dark red, dark purple, dark green. The darkness of the background brings out the shining beauty of the jewel. And don't we all have our fair share of darkness in life – losses, disappointments, mistakes, trials and tribulations? To accept and appreciate the darkness, to see the light better because of it, and to shine brighter as a result, that, dear friends, is perhaps the greatest art in life.

In *Hard Road to Wisdom*, Jesal Pankhania reveals fascinating human stories which confirm a hope-giving truth that wisdom teachers tell us – "**Where** you are doesn't define **who** you are." In this book, you'll encounter stories of individuals who have transformed problems into progress, pain into purpose, and adversity into prosperity. We will all be shrouded in the darkness of pain, problems, and adversity at some point in our lives, and preparing ourselves to face that with grit and grace is one of the wisest things we can do.

Jesal is inspired to introduce us to wisdom, which clearly has inspired and empowered his own life. He has experienced much in his own journey and is able to use that lens of wisdom to decode the deeper lessons from the lives around him. A famous adage tells us that small minds discuss people, average minds discuss events, but great minds discuss wisdom. May the hard road to wisdom that the individuals in this book traversed, educate and edify us in our own life journey. May we become wiser. May we shine even in a world that is often muddied with the darkness of imperfection.

S.B. Keshava Swami
Monk, Author & Thought Leader

Introduction

Hard Road to Wisdom is a book about finding hope within adversity and harnessing the power of transformation.

Based on interviews with real people and the extreme challenges they faced, I present my writing with the intent that you will be both humbled and inspired by the power of the human spirit.

Difficulties that unfold in the lives of Dheep Matharu, Robyn Travis, Ezekiel King, and Darren Chaplin are the central focus of this text. Exposing the power of confusion, fear, and desperation that crept into their lives, you will witness a greater power enter their lives instead: the tenacity to change.

As with many of us, there was a void in their lives and you will hear about how close they came to falling into the abyss beyond rock bottom. Compassion bloomed in my heart, for them and others in similar situations, and I hope it blooms in yours too.

Addiction, criminality, and violence littered their pathways, and in sharing their vulnerability and pain, I invite us all to wonder about the gateways into suffering and turmoil, to explore what more we can do to prevent or recover from such difficulty.

Anger, recklessness, and revenge punctured their lives allowing resentment, guilt, and shame to pour out of the wounds. Reaching a unique crescendo point, their lives sparked with transformation. As flames of change engulfed them, determination and resilience arose in their hearts, along with a yearning for a better life.

Listening to their stories, I emerged more empathetic and less prejudiced towards anyone walking a so-called unsavoury path. I question whether we give enough credit for the rare stem of wisdom that can sprout from those who have lived in reality's cold, harsh darkness. Emerging from the other side, they carry important insights rich with wisdom that are important to share.

Our Heroes earned wisdom, which is difficult to attain. However, through introspection, self-mastery, and perseverance, they removed chaos and confusion from their lives. It was clear to me that wisdom was a worthy pursuit, for it had brought illumination and clarity into their lives. Their stories now further inspire, giving hope to others.

Drawing upon my coaching, professional health-care experience, and love of Sanskrit and *yoga* philosophy, I explore wisdom: what wisdom is, what it means for us, and how it can be achieved. Ending the book with reflections on some invaluable gems and jewels of wisdom found along the curb side of this hard road, I attempt to get us to focus, not on what litters the path, but makes it glitter.

Learning from one's mistakes is wise;
learning from the mistakes of others is even wiser,
while not learning from any mistakes made is not wise at all.

Wisdom is certainly expensive, but ignorance costs a fortune.

So, with closed eyes, I recognise...
that I'm born into a dark state of ignorance and that wisdom
comes in many forms.

Through people and circumstances that open my eyes and fill
my life with light.
May I gravitate to that which gives me wisdom.

PART ONE

Heroes of the Human Spirit

Dheep Matharu

We have an inner and outer world. Success externally through popularity, position, prestige, and the accumulation of possessions does not bring real satisfaction and fulfilment to the life we live inside. Our first hero who had to traverse this hard road to wisdom is Dheep Matharu, and her story highlights this very contrast. The momentum of her career brought her to the bright lights of New York, the people's capital, the city that never sleeps, the place where dreams are made… as well as a few nightmares.

New York

Beginning with Chelsea Manhattan where art meets architecture, we witness the arrival of sunrise revealing clean pavements, well-kept stoops, and ornate railings that dress red-brown bricks, a classic of this part of New York. Sunrays light up vibrant street art that adorn the avenue's widest walls, evoking emotion, and stimulating thought. The aroma of coffee, bagels, and doughnuts rises to signal the waking of this city's people.

Within one such high-rise apartment, Dheep Matharu resided in her cove of hope and inspiration. She had everything: a rooftop deck, a private gym, and 250 square feet of modern New York to fill with her own story.

Carefully selected cushions of clashing textures embellished a cream-coloured couch draped with a contrasting black and white shawl.

Gazing out of her window at passersby, feeling a sense that she had 'made it,' there was an imperceptible truth that only Dheep knew:

"If you need cocaine every morning just to motivate you to have a shower and get to work, then obviously, there's something wrong."

Dheep's thoughts would oscillate between becoming a famous writer or designer on the one hand, while simultaneously feeling desperately lonely. She would regularly wish to die from taking an excess of drugs and, strangely, would notice the lack of ceiling fixtures carefully designed to stop people from hanging themselves. A rampant problem the city already possessed. Dheep considered herself sadistic for noticing this feature everywhere that she went.

Recounting having built up multiple layers of armour to protect herself, she proclaimed,

"I had finally made it, you know! I was in this big city, a high-flying fast *bitch* [laughing]. I also thought 'If I gave it all up and became an ordinary person, then who would love me?'"

Decorating her apartment to make it feel like a romantic movie, she attempted to play the leading role with photos, candles, unusual flower arrangements, Venetian masks, and cute, colourful ornaments. A huge walk-in closet brimming with expensive designer clothes obscured a furnished queen-sized bed caressed by grey silk. The fashionably astute would have recognised a $6000 Chanel purse and other extravagant items.

Dheep said she gave herself love and self-worth, but everything remained superficial. For, if you looked closely enough amidst the modern, clean look, you would see the faint evidence of powder cocaine across nearly every worktop or dresser. This was the classic case of a smiling face and a screaming heart.

The Facade

Recalling her beautiful apartment evidenced by a painful drug addiction, Dheep paused and closed her eyes before speaking her next sentence slowly and deliberately:

"I created a facade… to project who I should be… to be… admired."

This was a profound admittance by Dheep, and I reflected on how true this was for all of us. How many times do we act, speak, or dress in a way to satisfy the perception of others? How real is that perception, and how valid is it even? It is even more relevant when it comes to our posts on social media: Are we staying true to ourselves or simply pandering to the expectations of others? Are we deforming ourselves to fit the (unknown) perceptions of others? In Dheep's case, this was heightened due to her success. To the outside eye, she had everything: a six-figure salary and a lifestyle to match:

"But you see, I couldn't buy friends or relationships, which is what I inherently needed, and those who knew me were confused about why I was feeling depressed."

Accumulating possessions did not bring stability of the mind or satisfaction to the heart for Dheep, and her insight echoed the saying, 'We need to love people and use things, not use people and love things.'

Dheep recalled that her boyfriend at the time took an attractive portrait picture of her and merged it with a fake magazine cover:

"I loved that he thought of me as beautiful enough to be framed and hung on the wall. I had framed pictures of family and friends also, but I'd neglected them since moving to New York. They were there, frozen in time, but I couldn't remember the last time I'd had a meaningful conversation with any of them."

Loneliness, Pain, and Languish

Isolated, Dheep was using her friends and family to remind herself that she was loved and even worthy of love. Painfully unaware of the subconscious dialogue within her that was leading towards intoxicants, she now realises the pain was one of loneliness:

> "The drugs were my way of coping with an internal pain. Despite having many friends, I had very few connections, and I had this… this deep-rooted wound. I just hated myself."

Listening to Dheep I could sense that this contempt for herself was a constant wound that had kept reopening throughout her life. Dheep's story was not of drugs but of pain.

Early childhood is where her wounds began. Lacking connectivity, Dheep often felt like the odd one in her family, but could not determine why. She had an awareness of being alone and an inability to assimilate with her own family:

> "It doesn't have to be terrible abuse; it can just be that unconscious void that you feel at a young age. I just felt like the black sheep of the family."

Reinforcing this belief of loneliness by looking at life through a filter of 'not belonging,' she made her situation worse, and languish turned to anguish:

> "Beliefs and decisions at a young age - on a microscopic level - caused these ripple effects throughout my life. Actually, thinking about it, I was soft, naive, and shy,

and I would often feel uncomfortable when meeting people. These traits actually made me vulnerable."

Solemnly, Dheep detailed how this meant she could be easily manipulated and how she was bullied early on in life:

"I stopped doing regular things and meeting people… the right people you could say."

Reinforced by being scolded regularly, Dheep developed a version of reality in which her family did not love her, and no one was there for her. And it started to manifest.

I could sympathise directly with what Dheep was saying. My parents would regularly scold me and even hit me when I didn't meet their expectations. It was the same for my cousins and friends who were from the same background. Talking about it amongst ourselves was cathartic; sharing similar instances and laughing at our pain seemed to bring some relief. However, it was layered with a sense of abandonment, betrayal, or shame.

Now, through more mature eyes and having children myself, I can see the struggle of my parent's generation - a generation of immigrant Indians who looked very different to the host society. They were trying to navigate into a culture without losing their identity, provide an income without protest, and raise kids to succeed to their fullest potential.

But what was their measure for success? Where did their hopes lie? And what would happen if their children didn't meet these measures? Their dreams for success were to create professionals with degrees and attract the prestige, power, wealth, and prowess that naturally followed. We were a generation being rolled out like *roṭīs* to meet these metrics. Today's society is nourished by these efforts. While I've seen my generation, children of the Indian diaspora, account for a large number of professionals despite our overall low population, I have seen my generation stretched, pummelled, and painfully kneaded into shape. What have been the costs of our success? What might we have lost? Has anything deformed while we conformed to our parent's dreams? Becoming aware of the consequences of generational trauma, I ask the question: What does *real* success look like?

From Loneliness to Despair

Dheep's sense of loneliness led to internal pain. She started to drink alcohol at the age of 12 to numb her feelings. Rejection from relationships in her teenage years led to a deeper dive into her unholy trinity of alcohol, self-harm, and cigarettes:

> "When you break up from a relationship, it's not a new wound, it just presses on an old one."

Dheep was in full flow now, with amazing energy and admirable honesty, as she talked about realisations she had about herself. To me, it seemed like she had been on mute for so long but had now been given a mic; this story was about to take a turn for the worse.

Taking another extensive breath before entering another avenue of anguish, I gave her a moment to align her thoughts. Clearly, in some chaos from emotions that were orbiting her memories, she closed her eyes and released two large teardrops to the floor. Making a gesture with her right hand, she clasped her fingers as if grasping at a floating dandelion seed and brought it close to her chest. In doing so she seemed to capture herself. Centred and still, she now spoke with closed eyes.

> "I had a boyfriend who took drugs. I hated drugs. I thought it to be an unsavoury habit. I felt that 'drugs kill,' and so I told him, 'If you ever take drugs around me, I will leave you!'"

So then how did Dheep fall into a chasm of taking drugs herself? She recalls it to be amidst a deep and dark time of desperation. Dheep's loneliness served as a catalyst towards a bitter attempt at taking her own life:

> "It was a sure thing, an act full of conviction, but I awoke from the act with extreme pain and an inability to breathe. I don't know how I got back up the stairs to survive; I call it a miracle. I didn't have a sense of relief, joy, or thankfulness though - it was one of utter sadness."

It was after this unfortunate episode that she asphyxiated her boundary for drug-taking and made the choice to take drugs:

"My move to New York had been like finding a new playground - a move away from my family and my past."

Dheep had now befriended fearlessness. This new connection would push her to reckless degrees, bringing misfortune along a pathological pathway.

Dancing with Danger

Now, at the age of 27 and over a period of three years, Dheep's drug-taking habit had developed into a lethal cocktail severe enough to induce a heart attack. Although it began with trepidation, Dheep's habit gradually felt safer and safer and she took more and more, overdosing regularly:

"I started to consciously become a really unkind person. I felt like everyone treated me so badly, like... I'm never loved, so why even bother anymore?"

Dheep had become defensively toxic. Toxic to herself and others. She would treat men like dirt, sleep around, and try to make them feel as pained as she did inside. She had begun to use them for their money despite having more than enough money herself. Her lifestyle was like Jekyll and Hyde:

"I'd either engage in going out and going crazy or stay in with my intoxicants. My friends would invite me to go out and socialise but I would stay in with my safe, warm embrace of drugs and cigarettes."

Dheep admits that the security within her intoxicants was illusory. This mirrors many of the ways we attempt to numb or curb our attention away from our problems, like gently pruning the leaves of our issues while the roots grow deeper.

Fearlessness and Dysfunction

Dheep's cocktail was cocaine during the day and sleeping tablets at night. Her values and morals had gone completely out of the window. At times, she would order drugs at 10 o'clock in the morning while at work and take them back into a hyper-secure building, consuming them in the toilets:

"You see, I had no fear because I had tried to take my own life. I just couldn't seem to die. I would honestly try and try. I had no fear of going to prison; I just felt stuck. I couldn't escape my own life."

Arriving to work late, sometimes by as much as three hours, Dheep was given an informal warning by her manager. A major symptom of any problem with intoxicants is when daily function turns to dysfunction. Some people 'keep a lid on things' and remain a functioning addict, which is still certainly problematic, however, Dheep had gone beyond this now:

> "The clock was now ticking: I'd been given a time limit by when I needed to sort myself out."

Dealing with Human Resources, Dheep was potentially going to lose this incredibly sought-after, highly-paid position, and despite her hyper-fearless state, she still had one final fear.

The Final Fear

Lingering in the shadows of her mind was a fear that, in the end, she would be embarrassed by it all:

> "I was afraid of being found… with no life… lying with all my drugs."

Shaking her head gently, Dheep seemed to imagine her life coming to an end, tainted by an incomprehensible shame. Intelligently, however, she had already made a plan to mitigate this risk. Only a few people knew the extent of her drug taking and she made a pact with one of them:

> "I made him promise that if I *ever* died from an overdose, he would come into my apartment and clean up all the evidence of drugs from my life."

Dheep did not want her family to know of this addiction. She did not want drugs to be her story. Dheep seemed to value integrity and dignity. These values underpinned her plan to keep any drug-taking a secret. However, Dheep had now got to a point of exhaustion:

"I was tired of blacking out and this constant, constant cocktail of drugs."

* * *

My Own Misery

Dheep's story resonated with me. The truth is that I had been in a situation like this. A friend of mine had become a victim of his own secret addiction and died of an overdose. Being one of the few who knew him, I felt I had to go and clean up the house. The smell was terrible. Even though the forensics team had completed their clean-up, I still found a makeshift medical sharps bin in the cereal cupboard. Full to the brim with needles, this clear Perspex box revealed thin trickles of dry blood on the inside which seemed to whisper to me about a pain he had never revealed to anyone.

Normally, the house was clean and in aesthetic order. Each corner held memories of laughter, food sharing, and song. But now, it was a disorderly wreck with upturned sofas to match my upturned mind.

I shared this story with Dheep and she understood. Dheep helped me understand what my friend might have been feeling: the clouds of chaos and confusion that come with drug addiction.

I understood more, I empathised more, but still wished for more… more time with my friend.

My sincere conclusion is that Dheep's feminine energy saved her. Statistically, men seem much more aggressive in their attempts to take their own lives, bringing assurance and finality to their tragic yet liberating act.

Thankfully for Dheep, hope would arrive.

* * *

An Inner Voice

Dheep came to a point where she wanted to stop. She was completely ready for she had hit rock bottom:

> "On some days my clothes were mismatched which is a big thing for a budding designer [gently laughing]. My skin would break out into infections and I just became exhausted from feeling like this."

Describing how she 'checked in with her heart,' Dheep explained that she was ready to ask for help. Her request was internal, and so was the response. Through the mist of these drug-filled days, she reports an inner voice:

> "I call it an 'inner voice of wisdom' and refer to my recovery as an 'awakening.' Jes, I just got to this point where… I just… didn't want to die anymore.'

Shedding Skin

An intuitive inner voice requested her to shed layers of her identity. It was a painful process, but it allowed her to see who she had become:

> "I would say this voice was the universe, a higher power, consciousness, or that of God."

Receiving something indescribable, Dheep did not want to define it. I now sat enthralled, enlivened, and inspired.

In Sanskrit, one characteristic of divinity is *acintya* which means 'inconceivable' or 'indescribable,' and the turnaround that Dheep was going to make was nothing short of miraculous. Although anecdotal, this somehow shows that there is a guiding voice within us. I believe that we hold some intuition, logic, compassion, and insight we can tune into. I also believe that there are elements that are immeasurable, indescribable, and even beyond comprehension. Dheep continued,

> "This voice was telling me to leave my job and give away my possessions. It was a hard request and made for a very difficult yet mystical period of time."

Dheep was having a calling like the renunciates of Ancient India (Bhārat). I often wonder how society would function by re-recognising or normalising mendicants. There are always people who would benefit from living a monastic life, even if it were brief - a detox from the temporal.

I could see Dheep had had an awareness and experience similar to the *yogīs* and *saṃnyāsīs* who would give up all their worldly possessions. The society of Ancient India (Bhārat) would recognise these renunciates by the clothes they wore: cloth that was dyed with saffron to give a yellow-orange hue. However, as with all things meaningful, renunciation was more than the external dress. It was an internal way of being.

A young renunciate would have very few worldly responsibilities, and receive training and guidance while an elderly renunciate, having completed their duties to family and society, would retire to a simple life. They would have the support of an *āśrama* (spiritual centre) or a *guru* (spiritual teacher). However, Dheep was doing this raw, losing item after item along with parts of her false self:

> "I gave away $38,000 to friends, family, my ex-boyfriend, and homeless people. I reduced my possessions by shipping them off to various places. It was hard though, really hard… for me… to part with these things. They were my soul, my identity."

Dheep would sometimes curl up and cry with pain before giving away diamonds, jewellery, and bags that held values of $5000 apiece. Tears flowed as she felt like the identity that was adored by others was being torn apart. However, she knew these things were external, and that her internal resolve relied upon two important parts of the process: surrender and trust:

> "I became more self-aware. I looked at myself and thought, 'This is not how I want to live. I'm doing these things because I need love and I'm giving away my body and my sense of self to make lots of money... I'm selling my soul and not living virtuously.'"

Intrigued by this statement, I asked her for a definition of 'living virtuously.' She paused to think as I waited in silence. Valuing what Dheep might say having been through her struggles, I noticed her sit up a little straighter, and with a kind smile, she replied,

> "Living virtuously... It's doing the best that I can but knowing that I am not perfect."

I found it to be a liberating definition. Virtue always seemed so dogmatic and ideal - a bit sanitary, a bit too perfect. Here was a pragmatic, wise version of what a virtuous life could be. To be real, especially if you cannot meet the ideal.

Trust, Surrender and Hope

While still struggling with intoxicants, Dheep visited a church to help out at a homeless shelter. She described herself at that time as a 'hungry ghost,' constantly craving drugs and 'popping pills.' Conversing with a pastor while tears ran down her face, she exclaimed,

"There's so much suffering in the world and I don't know what to do!"

Their conversation developed into an earnest dialogue about trust and surrender. In doing so, she made more of a relationship with her inner voice, allowing for Dheep's awakening to become even brighter:

"I would even ask my inner voice, 'What's my purpose, what am I supposed to do?'"

Dheep explained that she allows this inner voice to guide her even today. Stripping away all the superlative aspects of her identity, she regularly quietens her mind and listens to that wise inner voice of rationality and reason:

"My inner voice helped create an awareness of deep wounds of the past and allowed me to access what was needed to promote healing. This inner wisdom was like a pathway guiding me to hope."

Dheep had gone to the ultimate place of darkness and despair: hopelessness. To lose hope is the tightest of clamps and the most subtle of vices. To become hopeless is to lose faith in life itself. To lose hope means to lose life. What do we have if we have no hope?

Contrastingly, to have hope is to have a zest for life. Therefore, hope is the greatest shelter, nutrient, and reason to live. Without hope, there is no chance of thriving in this world. Hope is the greatest of gifts and Dheep was finally receiving it.

Healing

Dheep's healing took time:

> "It's taken years to heal this false idea that I am alone, being able to trust people more. This inner wisdom has allowed me to know that we're loved, we are accepted, that we are whole, that we are here for a reason - that's what we ultimately want, right? I think this is why there is that laughing Buddha, because he is laughing saying, 'It's all within you.' We create all this... *stuff!*... the externals, while everything we need is just within us."

Dheep claimed that vulnerability is what helped in the process. She said she had to lay down various layers of armour and exchange a mass party lifestyle that was full of many superficial connections to an existence with fewer but more meaningful connections:

> "I mean, it's hard to say to someone, 'I felt like *this* when you said *that*,' and leave yourself open and vulnerable. But that's being real, and it's hard to be real, it's hard to be vulnerable. But when you do, you have two *real* people coming together in a relationship, not two facades, and then wonder, 'Why did they just suddenly fall away?'"

Dheep always had dreams of being a writer and has done so successfully releasing a series of books called *A New York Kind of Love: A True Story about Cocaine Addiction to Recovery*. Working with professionals who have developed an addiction to intoxicants, she connects with them and, in doing so, helps them connect better with themselves:

> "I help them connect with the inner wisdom of themselves, and in unlocking this one thing, it unlocks all other things."

From the language of Sanskrit, *dīpa* or *dheep* means 'light' and is the lexical source of the famous festival of lights, Dīvālī. Candles, or '*dheeps*,' are lit on the night when there is no moon, the dark night at the end of the lunar calendar.

This story is that of both the darkness and of light - Dheep.

Robyn Travis

We travel from the people's capital of New York to the culture capital of London and meet author and coach Robyn Travis, who graciously opened up to me about his hard road to wisdom. I felt immediately connected to his story, even though his background was Caribbean and mine was Indian, for we were both part of a diaspora living in Britain and had similar experiences. But, as you will see, his was very harsh.

Robyn has written a book titled *Prisoner to the Streets*, has a BA in youth justice criminology, a diploma in social work, and is a qualified boxing coach and mentor. However, getting here, Robyn walked a road littered with thorns and spilt with blood.

Intention

Remembering a childhood bright with inspiration, Robyn recounts wanting to be a footballer, but his teenage years were met with attrition. Opening up about the difficulties of his youth, he wanted the focus of our conversation to be on hope and change - hope for the next generation and deep, systematic change on an educational and institutional level. Robyn was speaking with me to collaborate for a better tomorrow.

Lost

Robyn's voice was deep but his words were deeper. Starting with a striking question, he caught me off guard and sobered me up quickly. This question immediately revealed just how adrift he was as a teenager:

"Do you know how far gone you are from reality, how *lost* you must be to be behaving like this?"

Pausing powerfully, waiting for an answer from me - although we both knew his question was rhetorical - he sighed and summoned memories and emotion from deep within himself and spoke an alarming truth:

"I wasn't able to be a child; my environment, my surroundings, and situation… all meant that I needed to be… planning murders."

Robyn's words shocked me, leaving me dumbfounded. Holding a degree of gravitas, he made my heart sink. He spoke of his confusion. A confusion he feels still exists for many teenagers in similar situations to this day:

"Many of the elements of my environment were setting me up for a life sentence, or even… death."

I wasn't ready for such honesty right off the bat. Passionately working like a man who is running out of time, Robyn got straight to the point and was already making an impact on me.

Quick wins over long losses

Recalling being around incredibly intelligent people who were street smart but, sadly, also myopic, Robyn stated,

> "Unfortunately, these people around me were short-sighted as to what aligns with a flourishing life. I have many stories where people tried to make quick wins over a long-term strategy."

I wondered about this type of environment, where prospects are few and far between, and the people surrounding you are stifling. What hope is there for anyone whose environment is swallowing them whole?

I remember reading an article named *Hunger Makes a Thief of Any Man,*[1] which correlated poor rice harvests to increased rates of crime. It made me wonder about scarcity. Environments of scarcity, or even the fear of scarcity, can create an anxious community resorting to desperate measures, self-centredness, and distrust. What can be done to begin to change these environments?

Care

Recalling very few people being truly positive or having real genuine care for him or his future, Robyn was wise to

---

[1] "Hunger makes a thief of any man": Poverty and crime in British colonial Asia. Kostadis J. Papaioannou. European Review of Economic History, Volume 21, Issue 1, February 2017, Pages 1–28

the fact that he had very little care or regard for anyone or anything.

"Those were turbulent teenage years for me…"

Insightfully, Robyn looks back and sees that he had not developed a language of care in his thoughts, words, or actions. Part of the reason for this was that he was not the recipient of the type of care needed to develop a caring nature:

"So when I say I didn't care, it's not because I was bad-minded and evil or anything like that, it's 'cause I had no one caring for me and I just wasn't able to care back."

Reflecting for a moment, Robyn explained how his mother, the primary caregiver in his life, was having to deal with significant life events. Robyn's father had been killed and the National Front (a far-right fascist political group of the United Kingdom) had fire-bombed their home:

"My mum had to put on a brave face whilst struggling amidst turmoil within. It's not fair on my mum to say I didn't experience any care; her mind was already broken before I was five. So she was broken on the inside…alone and trying to raise boys."

Discipline

Robyn and I both chuckled at similar experiences from our childhood when it came to obedience. Although he was Caribbean and I was Indian, we were both from immigrant families in England who were trying to pave some sort of path to security and achievement. Trying to acclimatise to the weather and assimilate with the culture, both our sets of parents experienced hardship and turned to heavy forms of discipline on us, their children, whom they felt needed to work hard and strive. This discipline often involved some physical violence:

I reflected on my own experience of being hit as Robyn talked of his:

"Me and my brother would get licks!… beatings!"

We both laughed therapeutically about getting 'straightened out' before school, but Robyn switched to a thoughtfully grave tone and spoke passionately about the consequences of such events:

"It's too early for that! A backhand around your face! Before 9 am! You would turn up to school *miserable*. And then somebody's gonna say the wrong thing to you, and you smack them as well. It's learned behaviour! The cycle's perpetual and it needs breaking with a conscious rethink."

Futility

We both smiled and nodded in agreement as Robyn moved the story along to when he finished school. Unaware at the time, Robyn thinks that a subtle depression must have hit him because he looks back and remembers feeling simultaneously lost, frustrated, and inadequate. With no mother to call on, he talked about feeling pangs of hunger as the evening approached:

> "I would think, 'What's the point in even makin' food, 'cause my food tastes like… well, it tastes like dirt."

My heart went out to him with this humble admission, and I lost concentration for a moment. Picturing Robyn on a dark evening feeling hungry and hopeless, the word 'dirt' kept echoing in my head. I could not fathom this experience. I enjoyed delicious nourishing home-cooked meals every single day. I wondered how many other 16-year-olds the school system fails by not giving them the skills to creatively cook a basic meal. How many other teenagers were going through this very same bleak experience?

Robyn's mind meandered before coming to education and how it could have truly served his situation:

> "It would have been good to leave school with some basic practical life skills like cooking. Understanding what access I had in terms of social support, you know,

a kid in my situation… I got myself into arrears when I didn't even know what arrears meant!"

Confusion and Clarity

Painfully unaware of the social support he could have had access to, Robyn feels the whole system, especially education, is lost and confusing. Robyn now works closely with teenagers and young adults from low socio-economic backgrounds and feels their needs are not met regularly.

Robyn feels the entire system requires a conscious rethink starting with classifying children as vulnerable because their minds have not reached maturity. He feels they cannot and should not be judged as adults:

"People are so divided currently that they do not *listen* to each other. All these distractions and disruptions in society mean people miss the most essential points about life."

With real-life insight, Robyn named this confusion as 'prisoner to the streets mentality,' explaining that there is a fundamental misconception involved:

"If something adverse were to happen to these teenagers and they don't retaliate, then they're perceived as weak individuals."

With concerns for current teenagers treading a similar path that he did, he continued compassionately,

"I feel for these kids, walking around with a knife - that's already a liability… Walking around with a gun - that's a five-year sentence in your pocket. Then you become worse when you're in each other's company. Because they're confused and you're confused. Then in all your confusion, you all become trapped… trapped together. Then what? You're all in jail living together, trapped at another level."

Robyn now runs workshops for teenagers and shares vital techniques which require subduing the ego, something we could all learn from:

"My workshops include how to deal with fear, how to really forgive, and how to apologise when you're wrong… because apologising… that takes courage."

Robyn has certainly walked a hard road to reach this point of credibility and connect with the youth.

Finding a dangerous friend in revenge
What follows is a situation that spiralled out of control, perpetuated by befriending a dangerous emotion: revenge.

Getting into a fight with a child much bigger than him, Robyn should have lost. Especially if it were based on size alone. But the boy did not win; Robyn did. A fair fight, one on one; Robyn's win dented the child's pride. Defeated, he returned in search of revenge:

"It hurt him, hurt his ego. Eventually, he comes back with what seemed like a thousand people and stabbed me. You see, I didn't even know it was him until weeks later. So I was planning to kill him, and kill him in the most silent of ways and get away with it. I was 16, so corrupted in my brain that I'm planning how to kill a person and get away with it."

Let's be honest, we're all susceptible to seek revenge at times, to harm someone who has harmed us. Feeling attacked, mistreated, or socially rejected, revenge feels like it could bring a sense of catharsis or closure.

We may not all engage in vengeance that grabs headlines or prison time, but retaliation in the shape of gossiping about a neighbour, scratching a car in the car park, or giving a poor customer satisfaction review all constitute revenge.

Revenge seems to repair our pain or lift our mood. However, the positive effects are fleeting, even after a few moments following a vengeful event. Soaked with ideas of revenge, a person might ruminate on their offender over and over again, allowing it to consume their mind.[2]

Alternatively, there is forgiveness, more complex and mature. Who is there for vulnerable children to weigh up

---

[2] Revenge: A Multilevel Review and Synthesis, Jackson et al, Annual Review of Psychology 2019 Jan 4;70:319-345]

this choice and model it for them? An angry reaction easily supersedes a patient response of kindness.[3]

Forgiveness, in the long run, re-humanises you after becoming a victim. Only now, after my own tussles with injustice and revenge and reading research around the subject can I say that there are three solid tangible benefits of forgiveness:

- Fewer reports of self-harm,
- A greater sense of belonging to the human community,
- A stronger sense of moral identity.[4]

No one was there to pass insights onto Robyn, but now he is armed with a Bachelor of Arts in Youth Justice Criminology. With the experience of an elder, Robyn spoke to me slowly:

"Hurt people… they *hurt* people. Revenge… it breeds revenge."

Scheming for revenge and making plans for violence, Robyn explained he was in a state of confusion in his youth as his tone turned to one of sorrow and regret:

---

[3] Carlsmith, K. M., Wilson, T. D., & Gilbert, D. T. (2008). The paradoxical consequences of revenge. *Journal of Personality and Social Psychology, 95*(6), 1316–1324.

[4] Schumann, K., & Walton, G. M. (2021). Rehumanizing the self after victimization: The roles of forgiveness versus revenge. *Journal of Personality and Social Psychology*. Advance online publication. https://doi.org/ 10.1037/pspi0000367

"I was torn between loyalty to so-called allies and my inherent compassionate nature."

This juxtaposition came to the forefront of Robyn's life with the death of someone he considered a friend. Robyn resonated with this person but they had to be counted as an enemy because of the different areas they lived in.

Robyn describes looking down at the blood on the floor knowing it belonged to his lifeless friend. Seeds of revenge began to fructify again:

"I'm thinking, 'Who killed him?' and then I'm shouting, 'Who killed him?' And then someone put their arm around me and was like, 'Yeah Rob, it was one of your boys.' And I realised in that moment, that I *couldn't* retaliate. I just couldn't be *angry*. I wasn't *allowed* to be angry at his death. But they'd killed someone I cared about and it made me realise I was… lost."

Sadly, this death paid part of the price for Robyn's liberation from delusion. At that moment, looking at the blood-stained floor, Robyn developed doubt. Doubt about the path he was taking. Robyn's quest for revenge turned inward, and he began to realise the need to change. Robyn admits that up until this point, he just did not care:

"I didn't care for my future, I didn't care about jail time, and, if I really think about it, I didn't care for myself."

A Catalyst for Care

As well as the unfortunate death of his friend, a second ray of light came in the form of purpose. A purpose outside and beyond himself in the shape of his unborn child. Bravely admitting that it did not come all at once, Robyn says it took its time to manifest and grow:

> "I know it sounds clichéd but I think my son's birth [thoughtful pause] didn't change me…but certainly made me think about things; it made me *start* to care."

Astutely aware of fathers who used their sons to sell drugs, Robyn was conscious that his son would either grow up resenting him or go down a similar road leading to death or imprisonment. I could hear the tension in his heartstrings as he thought back to these events for it was hard to fully complete his U-turn:

> "To hear the words, 'I'm pregnant,' I mean, I can't call it. I don't know what I'd be doing right now. And to be brutally honest with you, I didn't even love my child when my child was born because I didn't even know what love meant."

Startled by Robyn's honesty, it dawned on me that he was faced with the task of having to love and care for somebody when he was not even loving himself. Robyn's voice slowed again and turned to a whisper, affirming what I was thinking:

"And that's why these kids is killin' each other, 'cause, they, don't, love, themselves."

His words were soft, profound and erudite. We both let the silence digest our thoughts and I found both Robyn's gravity and honesty so severely sincere.

Circle of Care

Eastern philosophy, to which I am accustomed, firmly believes that we all have the potential for love due to the compassion innately within us. It is believed that to love, show compassion, or be devotional is a natural trait of our character, and Robyn is certainly no exception.

Suffice it to say that Robyn's circle of care has broadened boundlessly. Feeling genuine empathy for children and teenagers facing similar problems that he faced acts as rocket fuel for him. Robyn has put time and endurance into deep study and holds a bright vision that involves a total change in culture. To serve this purpose, Robyn has written a trilogy of books starting with *Prison to the Streets*, and has a strong desire for them to be studied as part of a school's curriculum. I am happy to report that this vision is slowly but surely becoming a reality.

Cultivating the Mind

Feeling that the current cultural climate is confusing children with disruption and distraction, Robyn wants to serve in a way that enables them to develop clarity about themselves and the world surrounding them. Robyn has two fears from his experience of diverse cultural groups living together. The first fear is the reduction of dialogue between these groups which causes divisive gaps to emerge despite being neighbours. Robyn's second fear is a turn towards hatred and violence, which occurs as hearts drift further apart.

My immediate thoughts at the time were on steering culture in a better direction. Asking Robyn whether it was pro-social behaviour we needed to focus on, Robyn agreed and emphasised the focus on grassroots-level change, where children become less vulnerable by equipping them with knowledge, especially subtle knowledge about the sciences of the mind:

> "I don't say it because it serves me but because it serves the people. My literature deals with anti-bullying, learned behaviour, childhood trauma, conflict resolution, seeing the bully as a victim, and more. I had a bully: he was from Somalia, he had a scar on his face, and he would want to fight me on Monday through to Friday. But I can see now with clarity that he is actually a victim. For him not to become a bully from his experiences would be abnormal."

Believing this process can start with an introduction to simple concepts at primary school will serve children well. Robn feels that layers of complexity can be added during education in the teenage years as dialogue matures.

Revolution in Education

Passionate about education, Robyn feels that a real revolution for children would be a major way of redressing the imbalance in their lives:

> "There's education, and then there is *real* education - real in that it has meaning, relevance, and practicality; that then leads to purpose in life."

I understood what he meant. Some schoolchildren need stability and security, while others, who are in a more comfortable position, move on to topics of thriving and flourishing. Not everyone is served by a one-size-fits-all approach.

What if educators could decide more locally how best to teach those in a certain area? Is that too radical or too decentralised, requiring too much work? Do the children of the next generation not deserve a re-invention or rethink?

Thinking back to my own teenage years I remember having a friend who did not even have carpets in his house. He constantly talked about wanting to help his mum earn. We were fourteen years of age and would regularly walk to school together. Both he and the teaching staff were left miserable with nearly every interaction day after day. He needed food, warmth, and a toothbrush. Unfortunately, he turned to selling drugs and then started taking drugs, and eventually, I heard the unfortunate news of his overdosing while in prison a year later. He had an entrepreneurial spirit and I still think about how his life would have been different if it had been channelled differently.

I asked Robyn what he would say to someone in charge of education, to which he replied,

> "The system could try and have a way of looking at what is missing in the life of a child... in their home life. Then empower them by realising what they are lacking... then work collaboratively to give them healthy experiences to provide what they lack."

To me, this seemed like worthwhile work but would require an overhaul of the entire system - a system with a more local approach based on the needs of the area. If there are tensions between communities then a school education can build bridges. If an area has low economic growth then this is the fundamental knowledge-need of the area. A new mindset would be required with a long-term vision, always questioning how we best serve the children, especially the most vulnerable in terms of unstable, insecure, and dysfunctional home lives.

Robyn's Work
A huge part of Robyn's work is speaking directly to teenagers. These teenagers are too young to be in prison but have committed crimes that mean they are spending time in what people may call juvenile detention centres or secure units, all euphemisms for a teenage prison:

"We gotta fix children, not criminalise them for their actions… we have to re-educate them on things they're simply not getting at home… I connect with them but it's bittersweet."

Some of these kids might be facing one or two decades of imprisonment and for Robyn, this is a source of frustration. One teacher at a facility explained Robyn's sessions to be,

"both heartbreaking and inspiring at the same time… Robyn was able to connect with them and lift their opinions of themselves and open their eyes to the potential inside them."

Airwaves

The Prison Radio Association has been regularly broadcasting Robyn's work across the nation giving access to Robyn's literature which aims to give hope and inspiration to all who tune in.

The Sanskrit language has the term *vijñāna* which means "realised knowledge," and Robyn represents this when dealing with children and teenagers who arrive at school with a harsh home life. When people with *vijñāna* speak about their experiences with wisdom, then people naturally listen. Speaking about his life, Robyn connects with the teenagers in these units, and I wonder what would happen if he were to connect with them earlier and how we can make this happen. How can those with realised knowledge connect with those who need it most? Is it discriminatory to seek out pupils in need, or is it intelligent discernment?

Incidentally, my own father worked in one of these units as an educator for a decade. I had visited twice to give workshops on yoga and meditation during their multi-faith days and I can admit that it is a challenge to connect and build rapport. However, I can see how Robyn's honesty, sincerity, compassion, and wise words would connect with teenagers, proving that certain people are right for a given circumstance. So I am happy to amplify Robyn's voice.

Robyn is very passionate about ensuring that children who commit crimes should not be criminalised or demonised. He feels they should be allowed to re-enter society without a criminal record. His words resonated with me again. We mature at different rates and that all-important pre-frontal cortex matures in our mid-twenties. Instead, we have socially debilitated individuals who end up being sentenced to life even when they leave prison:

> "Anyone under the age of 18 cannot be called a criminal. They are too young, too immature, and if they come out with a criminal record they can't assimilate into society. We need to prevent rather than intervene."

The words were not new to me: 'prevent rather than intervene.' Being a dental health professional our mantra was always 'prevention is better than cure,' but this was way beyond tooth decay; this was prevention of a whole portion of our young generation rotting. Are they not part of the whole? Or are we happy just extracting them from society?

Robyn was right. Despite the sweet exchanges and the connection he makes with these criminalised teenagers, Robyn is all too aware that they have gone past the point of prevention. Hoping his book can provide some much-needed prophylaxis, he vented,

> "That's my frustration, Jes… sadly some of them are too far gone… My dream is to see my book in the schools, taught on the curriculum and empower the kids to understand these important life skills on behavioural management and anti-bullying."

Robyn's mind seemed to reel back to the lost and almost hopeless 16-year-old he was when he left school. Hunger and his lack of skill in the art of cooking now fuel a hopeful revolution, an overdue revolution of education and social care.

After speaking with Robyn, I got a sense that he wanted an education system that is designed by the educators in collaboration with the child's caregivers. By considering the child's homelife closely, there is more chance of an education system producing less futility:

> "They get what they need for where they're at and where they are coming from."

Clearly, this takes more work, and the education system would need to slow down. But what better way to nurture an investment if not with greater care and attention? Children are the best investment for our future. This may not seem like equality but it does seem equitable.

Robyn's wishes

It was hard to stop Robyn now; he was in full flow, I was just absorbing his passion:

> "I hope for an education system that cultivates teenagers to be able to adapt to the world and not feel like they've hit a brick wall or entered a void. I want teenagers to develop economic literacy, an ability to market themselves, start up a business, know about taxes, and more… those are my wishes."

Robyn then shared with me something more remarkable than his book. Robyn's bright mind had developed a game which simulated dealing drugs with the aim of getting out of the 'game' by becoming legal:

> "It helps them learn without it becoming a preaching sermon… they learn by experience."

One London school included Robyn's book in its teaching curriculum, and he hopes it will be included in many more.

Final Metaphor

Being a deep thinker, Robyn enjoyed contemplating a metaphor I offered him. The metaphor is of two prisons that exist on the road to wisdom.

One prison lies along the path of abundance where success and virtue glitter the way, creating a psychic prison. Here, self-righteousness and arrogance shackle us.

The other prison lies along the desolate path where vice can manifest, especially in desperate attempts for survival, thus encasing us in shame, guilt, victimhood, and resentment.

We talked more about how both virtue and vice are avenues towards wisdom, how the sanitary righteous road of virtue leads to fame, while the hard road of vice leads to infamy.

This dichotomy splits judgments. The desolate can become clouded by inferiority complexes, shame, guilt, and anger, while the abundant can fall into the trap of swimming in conceit, superiority, and exploitation.

In truth, however, both avenues lead to a greater place: wisdom. Wisdom is a place where the shackles are broken and the clarity is sharp and bright. In Sanskrit, this would be a state called *viveka*, which means clarity and wisdom.

Concluding our conversation, which went far over the time we had allotted, Robyn pointed out how vice, being destructive, can lead to more vice, while virtue can *also* lead to vice in subtle or inconspicuously deceitful ways.

Agreeing that both prisons were traps we needed to avoid, we agreed to stay humble so we could continuously move towards wisdom. Knowing what to do at that moment in the right way, is the essence of another Sanskrit idea: *dharma*.

> "I like that... two paths to wisdom... if I can't argue with it then I like it... I like things that make me think. I also understand that I myself can still become a prisoner to these psychic prisons also... so it's a continuous process; the work never ends."

Throughout my interview with Robyn, I found his wisdom and humility clearly evident. Despite being an expert in his field, he was not arrogant or boastful, but caring, compassionate and deliberate in his thoughts.

Robyn's literature, expertise, and passionate words of wisdom soothe people going through dark winters, help them move into the spring, and allow knowledge to bloom brightly.

Ezekiel King

The *Bhagavadgītā* chapter 3, verse 35, states that seemingly positive character traits, if placed in the wrong situation, can become a vice. We see the traits of courage, audacity, and curiosity come into play in the life of public speaker and author, Ezekiel King. Ezekiel's greatest need as a teenager was for inspiration and guidance to channel these traits of his. Although they did eventually turn up and transform his life's trajectory, it was after years of toil.

Breathing in: Inspire

Inspiration strikes us in different ways. It might be the wonder of beauty within nature or an emotive speech. However, for Ezekiel King, it was in a state of desperation that he found his. Empty and desolate, Ezekiel sat in a dull and dingy prison cell tasting and smelling the stale, damp air that lingered around him.

Discomfort grew greater in every moment as the pale blue walls with their dark grey lines seemed to close in on him. Ezekiel's ease reduced with every minute that passed, and his sadness deepened after every second. Looking into the distance while speaking to me, Ezekiel felt those moments again and spoke quietly:

"I just sensed… an increasing distance from home."

Imprisoned for the third time, he was facing twenty years in jail. So this time he felt isolated and desperate:

> "I was thinking... something *has* to change. And if I am *lucky* enough or *blessed* enough to earn my freedom back in the near future, something has to change."

In the prison cell, Ezekiel began to think objectively. With laser-sharp acuity of this adverse situation, Ezekiel decided to look for truth.

The Energetic Child

Looking back Ezekiel remembers being a good child. At the age of ten, he has memories of being a well-behaved and intelligent child who was excelling academically. Entering secondary school with a strong energy about him, he was deemed as mischievous and disruptive, quickly labelled as 'naughty' by the teachers. I sensed Ezekiel's tone change as he spoke of this as an injustice:

> "Looking back, I can now see that I was being singled out. Rather than being viewed as the kid who needs help, some support, and direction, I was reprimanded instead... time and time again. Now I can see with hindsight that I needed my energy channelled - some more ambition, and certainly more intrigue. That's what I needed. I can see it now."

He was expelled in his first year at secondary school as dialogue between himself and his school broke down along with their relationship. Two years later, he was expelled again, and at the age of fourteen, Ezekiel found himself in his third school. Reliving these memories, I could sense his struggle as he wrestled with a dilemma he faced at such a young age:

> "I really wanted to knuckle down in this third school because I believed, even back then, that I wasn't a bad person. I just didn't have people in my network to enable me to excel or really promote positive success in my life."

Ezekiel's career in school was taking a nosedive, but how he left school with an honourable set of exam results was down to a remarkable exchange with a wise teacher. Stumbling upon each other in the corridor, this teacher took it upon himself to motivate Ezekiel in the right way:

> "What this teacher did was essentially psychologically manipulate me to do well [laughing]. He said, 'You're so intelligent that you're going to be your own worst nightmare.' He told me I would leave school with nothing and so he challenged me... and I thought, 'I'm going to prove you wrong.' He knew that I responded well to challenge."

Research shows that around 10% of the population has a dominant character trait, and they need challenges to motivate them. This illuminated teacher was clearly sensitive to Ezekiel's inherent need for challenge, even if he was not aware of it himself. Such a strong role a wise teacher can play.

Broad-minded teachers who could see a situation from many perspectives were called *munis* during the Vedic period of ancient India.[5] This flexible multi-perspective ability meant that they could give counsel correctly according to time, place, and circumstance. In his *muni*-like way, this teacher squeezed the right type of pressure at the right moment to allow Ezekiel to leave school with something in his bag.

A Career in Drugs

If only this same teacher were able to have Ezekiel's ear after his school years, for it was during these summer months that he tasted success in something else: illegal drug money.

School ended, the summer passed, and college began. Ezekiel was proving himself very bright as he pursued a career towards becoming a chartered accountant, excelling in his exams and proving to be the top in his class. However, Ezekiel had made liquid cash over the summer and he compared the predicted salary of a chartered accountant years down the line to the drug money he could make with more immediacy:

---

[5] Bhagavad Gita As It Is Chapter 2 Verse 56, AC Bhaktivedanta Swami, 1968, BBT Publishing

"I thought, 'Why am I sitting here for four years when all I need to do is double what I sold last week and I'm already making £50K a year.' So… I paved the way to my own destruction."

Although the comparison was intellectual, it was also myopic. Losing the drive for his accounting career, he focused his energy on exponentially growing liquid cash that he was making from drug deals.

Pocket Money

The beginning of that summer started with Ezekiel wanting a little play money to simply enjoy the long warm summer days, so requested his mother to give him some pocket money. Requesting £15 one day and then again the next, his mother responded by saying she simply could not afford to give him that amount of money every day. Clearly upset by this, Ezekiel tried to threaten his mother by saying he would 'rob the post office' if she couldn't give him money over the summer. Unable to have his financial needs met, Ezekiel was left with a bright scheming mind. Reflecting on a crossroad that had presented itself during this poignant summer, Ezekiel stated:

"I just think about what I really got out of school… how it failed me to be honest… think about it… in the ten years that someone's at school, by the end, they just *have* to leave with a tradable skill. If not, how do they negotiate with the world when they've got desires?

If I was a high-level tiler, plasterer, or plumber I could have earned £150 a day, good clean honest work… that would have been enough for me to just chill that summer, and spend the cash I'd earned."

He was right. Many students feel this same dissonance about their secondary school education. How does it not translate into assimilation into the real world? Ezekiel could have earned honestly and ecologically that summer had he left with a tradable skill. He would have had money for recreation without needing to beg off his mum or threaten to 'rob the post office.' Reflecting on how impressionable this time of his life was, Ezekiel continued:

"If I could go and speak to my fifteen-year-old self during that summer… hmm… I would've said, 'Get a trade, look at property, make friends with kids from more affluent regions of the city… don't mix with kids that are gang-bangin' and selling drugs."

Perfect Storm

A lack of tradable skills, a strong desire for fun times during a free summer, and an innate level of curiosity, courage, and audacity created the perfect storm for a road into criminality. Many elements were against him: his environment, his association, his desire, and now he carefully contemplated his means. Ezekiel and his friend tallied together all the money they had and bought as much cannabis as they could, bagging it and selling it to double their profits.

£500 per week turned to £1000 which, mixed with their financial illiteracy, caused another problem to manifest:

> "I spent at the same rate as I earned. But I had no understanding of financial management, savings, or investing. I just knew how to make liquid cash, and how to spend and *waste* liquid cash. The weed turned to cocaine, the cocaine turned into guns, robberies, and violence, and it wasn't long before I ended up in prison."

This was incredibly disappointing for me to hear. Do students leave school with any understanding of income, expenses, banking, loans, credit cards, and so on? Do they even know the basics of home economics?

Thinking in More than One Dimension

When faced with adversity, Ezekiel, being a natural problem solver, readjusted time and time again but admits he was looking at singular actions and singular events:

> "I would think, 'I'm in jail for robbin'... kilos of methadone... so... just don't do any more robberies, just stick to selling cocaine.' Then something would go wrong in that department and I would make an

adjustment there. I just didn't understand that there was something wrong with the whole picture."

It was during this third visit to prison and facing those blue and grey walls closing in on him that Ezekiel finally thought:

"Something is really really wrong here… something really has to change."

Considering the rate at which we mature, the role of one part of the brain is important here: the prefrontal cortex. Among other things, it helps an individual predict the consequences of their actions, anticipate events in the environment, control impulses, and manage emotional reactions. It does not fully develop until a person is around twenty-five years old.

Here, we see Ezekiel being forced to consider his actions and reactions, his fate both now and in the future. In a Vedic society, *karma* is central to growth and understanding. Ezekiel was looking at his role in his own karma:

"Twenty-seven years old and with children that depended on me, I was now looking at being in a prison cell and never leaving it. I started to look at my life objectively, so I took myself out of this entire situation and began to look at my problems as if they belonged to someone else."

Sometimes, in my coaching sessions, I ask, 'What would the wisest person you know tell you here?' The responses can be incredibly insightful. This is especially true because you do not actually ask the wise person; you take on their mindset. In doing so, you tap into your inner wisdom, and Ezekiel did this at that very moment. He tapped into his inner wisdom.

Aspiration

It was during this time that he began to consider people he could aspire to be like. He considered businessmen like Lord Sugar, Peter Jones, Richard Branson, and Duncan Bannatyne, and started to make comparisons:

> "I would think, 'Why do their bank accounts say 20, 30, 40, 50 million and I have a sheet in my hands that says I'm only allowed to spend £47.50 in the prison canteen?'"

Ezekiel started to coach his own mind and advise himself that these people were not immersed in a world of drugs, guns, and violence; instead, they were publishing books, owning percentages in high cash-generating businesses, and had investments that earned them high passive incomes:

> "I realised that these role models had very high levels of financial management and a robust network. I desired

this sort of change in my life, but trapped in a prison cell, I wondered what I could actually do."

Seeing some potential in Ezekiel, a fellow prison inmate inspired him:

"It was an Iranian man who held a doctorate in Engineering. He recognised an ability in me... an ability of vivid storytelling and advised me to write a book."

The Journey Within

With a newfound purpose, Ezekiel began an intense inward journey. A journey many fail to take, a journey through layers of dirt and dust that accumulate on the mirror of the mind. Facing our misgivings, our mistakes, and our misfortunes is a large part of coming face-to-face with ourselves. For Ezekiel King, this journey turned out to be a deep therapy, slowly stripping away falsities and exposing difficult truths:

"I sat in my prison cell with a dictionary and thesaurus and for one year straight I wrote, by hand, 350 sides of A4. And *now*, that book is internationally published and is called *From Innocence to Arrogance*."

Admiring his journey I questioned his mind and state of being as he went on this journey, and my instincts were correct: this intense mental expression came at a cost:

"I was physically ill in bed. I suffered severe chronic headaches for over a week; the agony was relentless. I'd taken myself back to incredibly emotional moments in my life. I went back to my fifteen-year-old self and tried to work out what the true reality of my situation was."

Ezekiel King wrote in the first person vocalising his thoughts and feelings, deeply reflecting objectively:

"I reflected like this for such a long time that it literally left me physically ill in bed for a whole ten days. I couldn't eat, go to the gym, or even open my eyes. I just focused on hydrating myself until this relentless pain passed naturally."

Emergence

King emerged from his introspection realising that he had been overriding and ignoring a voice within his head and heart, a voice that constantly told him he was doing wrong:

"I believe we all have this inner voice but we tend to dismiss it. We shouldn't dismiss it though… we should listen. I didn't have guidance from outside to validate this inner voice… to tell me something was immoral or wrong, and now [long pause] I just want to save lives, Jes."

Slowing the pace of his words, King seemed to speak to me with the gravity of a sage. He shifted his attention onto his own children and the next generation, realising he had a duty to help them tune into their own inner voice of reason.

Believing in the potential and ability a child has, King thinks that early on in primary school, children can be taught a suitable way to tune into this inner voice of reason. Reflecting on important conversations he had with his young daughter, his tone switched to a soft, caring, and patient one. He mimicked his own voice in the tone required when speaking to a tender heart:

> "I said to my daughter, 'If you give or sell something to someone that is dangerous to them or can harm them, then that is very very bad. Because you are destroying that person.' Then I questioned her about what things she thought were dangerous and harmful... we had a little dialogue. Then I asked her, 'Do you know what drugs are?' I described them to her in a suitable way for a child to understand and finally asked her, 'Would you ever sell drugs to anybody?' She said, 'No daddy, no.'"

This was endearing. In Sanskrit, the word for duty is *dharma*, and when a person aligns with this, they find fulfilment. *Dharma* encompasses purpose, ability, and responsibility. For King, he had a purpose outside of himself; he was aligning himself with his *dharma*.

Inner Compass

King rubbed the lower part of his face and pursed his lips. His sombre look told me he was trying to give his children an opportunity to develop something he had not: an internal moral compass. Strong character traits meant he could climb hierarchies and reach success, but his internal compass had become demagnetised in the misguided curiosity of his youth.

Talking fondly of his son, King wanted to empower him with critical thinking and the ability to make healthy choices:

> "I'll give my son choices… A or B. I've shown him a heroin addict's house and a nice conference room and I'll say, 'You want to do your business here or here?' I want him to be smart… apply himself… make the right choices in life."

Clearly attuned to the fact that a drop of experience is worth more than hours of theory, King feels strongly about a true and wholesome education which allows children, especially from lower socio-economic backgrounds, to develop a network of role models:

> "Leaving school without basic trade and financial management skills is tragic. If kids who lacked role models were put in front of a professional dentist like you or a public speaker like me, and we met at regular

intervals over a few years, I am sure we could help them do some really great things with their lives."

Growing up on a council estate and mixing mainly with the have-nots, King realised he had developed a frame of mind and a set of habits centred on scarcity, desperation, and hopelessness. His energy rose, and his passion became evident, breaking into a compassionate monologue:

"These kids are actually killing each other Jes!... [pause]... Murdering each other on the side of the street... and they won't listen to anyone. I want to talk to them because everything they aspire to do, I have done: own a gun, sell kilos of coke, discharge firearms. It won't impress me and it won't scare me because I know we need to have this conversation. And then hopefully... hopefully, I can avert them from a prison sentence or an early grave. So that's my purpose if you like."

Outside of Ourselves

King gets through to them and they listen because he speaks from experience and a genuine position of care. It takes time and patience but he offers them a possibility that success lies elsewhere:

"They need to come in contact with something outside of themselves which is positive and inspiring."

Unknowingly and inadvertently, King echoed the philosophy of beauty and aesthetics and the ideas of Mary Myatt. Her vision is a new direction for education,[6] and the philosophy emphasises the need to surround children with beauty to leave them in awe. These awe-inspiring moments create an internal impetus.

Additionally, there is a *Sanskrit* term, *ākarṣaṇa*, which means 'magnetism' or 'attraction' and is one of the names for divinity known as Kṛṣṇa. The idea here is that divinity is so beautiful that being exposed to it inspires within us the need to be the best version of ourselves, the highest expression of ourselves, and thus live an inspired life of love and devotion to whatever leaves us in awe. Be it nature, the universe, relationships, or the harmony of society.

Drive

King feels that the world needs to hear the stories that are within him and has finished a second book called *A Villain's Journey*. Time and time, again he comes out of his comfort zone to strive for something beyond himself. Reflecting maturely on his past and how it links to his future hopes, he told me:

"Maybe I didn't have it in me at 15 *not* to sell drugs. Maybe I had to walk this hard road. Maybe I couldn't just talk with affluent people to build my network but

---

[6] Curriculum Conversations between subject and senior leaders. M Myatt, J Tomsett. John Catt Publication, 2021

hopefully, someone else can learn from the stuff I've been through."

Theodore Roosevelt famously said, 'To educate a person in mind but not in morals is to educate a menace to society.' King, now holding a position of inspiration to society, painstakingly educated himself in morality despite the trappings of his youth, an unbridled mind, and a fraught education.

Darren Chaplin

Regularly my academic rival, Darren Chaplin was in nearly every single one of my classes from the first day of secondary school to sixth-form college – from the sciences, mathematics, our tutor group, the arts, and physical education. Fierce but friendly foes academically, we shared the same wit and our humour would often get us into trouble. I was there during his first fight when he launched an apple point blank into another boy's head, and he was there for me with words of solace after my multiple run-ins with the neo-Nazis that attended our school. Journeying into and out of a gambling addiction that almost consumed him, he tells his story in the hope that it gives hope to others in the same situation or prevents others from walking the same path.

Early Days

Maturing early and having an older brother meant he would hang about in pubs and 'do more adult things' in the evenings and weekends. Darren even helped me to get one of my first jobs as a waiter in my late teens and our competitive streak continued as we tallied up our tips at the end of a shift.

Naturally, our lives diverged, but we would still keep in contact using social media, liking each other's pictures, or making a few comments here and there. However, some twenty years after those more innocent, care-free days, we protected some quality time to talk, and Darren started with a strong critique of himself:

> "You can have all the skills in the world but if you don't know what to do with them, you're not *taught* what to do with them, or *fundamentally* what is right and wrong, then it's of no use. What's the point of your skills and intellect?"

Darren's insight echoes Comenius, a man who many consider to be the father of European education. John Amos Comenius democratised education in the 16th century and stated:

> "To educate in skills and intellect but not morality is like putting a sword into the hands of a madman."

We will see the power of gambling and how mad it can make us through Darren's story.

A Malleable Age

Teenagers can be moulded, which is both good and bad. If the skills and intellect are not rooted in an internal moral anchor, then life quickly spirals out of control. These skills can mislead one down slippery dark alleyways. Darren, clearly intelligent, talked about how his addiction began:

"I've always gambled, from say 15, 16 years of age, but just like any addiction, it snowballs and snowballs and gets out of hand. What starts with a couple of pounds here and there turns to 10, then 20."

Reminiscing about a slot machine he would play on, he explained his strategy. The machine had a £15 jackpot. Darren would start by putting in £5, then another £5, followed by another £5. Now a win would mean he would only break even at best:

"I would think, 'It's *gotta* drop in a minute.' It's a hope that you're gonna get your money back… but then you're *also* thinking, 'I don't want someone else to come along and win *my* money.' When you think like this, Jes, then you have to realise that you're trapped."

Here within lies the entanglement of the situation. Darren went from wanting to win £15 to then needing to break even and finally trying to avoid the anguish of seeing someone else come along, put in a single coin, and win 'his' money. The reality is that once Darren staked that money, he had to accept that the money was not his anymore. When it didn't come back, he had to accept it as lost. But because he wasn't doing so, he was losing himself in the process. This is gambling in a nutshell: quickly turning from hopeful to desperate.

What did Darren do? He continued, despite having no chance of a compelling result:

"I'd think, 'Well now I've put 20 in to get back 15, so I'm 5 quid down.' When you get to this point, Jes, to win simply to minimise your losses, you should realise that actually you're never gonna win now."

Fire of Desire

The Bhagavadgītā, an enlightening conversation between a warrior and his charioteer before an epic battle, discusses the transmutations of desire. The charioteer, Kṛṣṇa, is extremely wise, and the warrior, Arjuna, desperately needs enlightenment. Kṛṣṇa describes various inner enemies on the path of progress, such as selfish desire, anger, greed, arrogance, and envy.

Transposing these onto the emotions of a gambler, especially the delicate mind of a teenager, makes for an interesting illustration.

Seemingly innocent desires to turn £1 into £15 are harmless single flames; add a small dose of greed to fuel them, and the flame quickly turns into a much bigger fire of desire.

Envy comes along and whispers, 'Now… you don't want someone else to come along, place a single £1 bet, and take all of your winnings, do you? How would you feel if that happened?' Thus, the gambler carries on, despite being down, just to avoid the arrogance of ego being bruised.

By the end, this cocktail has produced a burning inferno that turns everything to ash.

Same game, bigger stakes

Remarking that he won as much as £28,000 one day, Darren explained that in a couple of days, it was all gone:

"This money was enough to clear my debts at the time. You see there's this buzz, you might win big and everything's rosy, but as it goes on it doesn't work like that. The more you win, the more you bet, the more you stake."

Hearing the word 'stake' made me consider what we sacrifice while gambling. Consciously, we gamble an amount of money we are willing to risk, but there is also an unconscious sacrifice. Shortcuts to victory are alluring but their joys often do not last as long as the success that required considerable effort. Wins acquired cheaply are often tainted with a lack of fulfilment which can expand the void within, instead of filling it.

With bets going from £1 to £10 to £100s, I asked Darren how aware he was of the impact of raising stakes and losing big, and what happens to the power of reasoning. Darren explained:

"You always see the odds and you can always work out what you may or may not win, but in the end, it's rationality that you lose; it goes out the window."

In this regard, there is another interesting term Kṛṣṇa mentions in the Bhagavadgītā which is *vikarma*.

Understanding *karma* as the law of 'what goes around, comes around' is commonly understood, but what is *vikarma*?

Vikarma sees an individual having a sense of cause and effect but wants to bypass, avoid, or shortcut the process. Swami Bhaktivedanta comments on this path of *vikarma* as the 'royal road to hell.'[7] He means hell in the sense of a hellish existence in mind and spirit where everything is toxic, dangerous, or destroyed in the end. Is this not what happens to unfortunate gamblers?

Kṛṣṇa explains that these emotions, if unchecked, can lead to *buddhi-nāśa* or delusion.[8] Delusion, depicted by darkness, is a movement away from wisdom, which is represented by illumination. Within darkness, we do not know where we are, who we have become, and in which direction to turn. It is in this delusion that we lose our rationality and reasoning power, wandering deeper into the darkness.

At this point, Darren's world had become vikarmic in nature, as he constantly tried to bypass the laws of cause and effect and minimise his losses altogether. Removing his sense of rationality, muffling his morality, and dampening his intelligence, he spiralled further downwards.

---

[7] Bhagavad Gita As It Is, Chapter 16 Verse 4, AC Bhaktivedanta Swami, 1968, BBT Publishing.

[8] Bhagavad Gita As It Is, Chapter 2 Verse 63, AC Bhaktivedanta Swami, 1968, BBT Publishing.

Bereft

With a bright mind bereft of rhyme and reason, Darren, with delusion and despair, surveyed the depth of his debts. Accumulated through credit cards, payday loans, and his hard-earned cash, he was down £45,000 – a far cry from trying to recover £15 from that initial slot machine that left him fruitless. Darren's gambling habits had led him into darkness, and within this darkness, he had lost hope. With two young children and a loving wife, he saw no way out:

"This is how far into despair gambling drove me… to suicide. I didn't see a way out, so I thought… just end it."

My heart skipped a beat as I heard Darren utter these words. It then sank as I listened to the details:

"I left a note for my wife detailing what I had done… took a bag of pills, and drove off in my van."

Sitting in a lay-by, Darren hopelessly saw no way out and was willing to offer his very soul into oblivion. Oblivious to Darren's level of suffering, I felt my eyes widen as he spoke, and a lump in my throat appeared as I wondered how this was going to unfold:

"So… someone we knew was driving by, recognised my van, and messaged my wife… saying, 'Your van's down there.' thankfully my wife got it... she got the message."

Darren explained that his wife rushed to his side with their children before he could take a single pill.

The silence was sobering.

My friend, a bright, witty, and intelligent lad, with whom I had spent nearly every school day, had been driven to the depths of despair. Bereft of all hope, he was saved by a text message.

Darren let there be silence, knowing I was thinking. My thoughts were, 'What if that man decided to send the text a little later, what if his wife didn't read it in time, what if she didn't know which lay-by... what if, what if, what if?!'

I pursed my lips and narrowed my eyes as Darren eventually curled a smile at me, and we both sighed. Shaking my head, I broke the silence:

"Mate... I mean, some might say that was divine intervention."

Following our witty contradictions of each other, Darren responded,

"It was... lucky. The odds must have been in my favour"

I shook my head, trying not to laugh at this casual comment about such a deadly situation, but it was hard not to. This was Darren through and through. We both laughed like awkward school boys as men often do at uncomfortable truths. Darren could always make a situation lighter with his humour. Humbled, Darren relayed his gratitude for his wife finding him, saving him, and ultimately supporting him through a path of recovery.

All Bets are Off

Darren attended a Gamblers Anonymous meeting the very next Monday and has been clean of his gambling habit for a number of years now. He went into a debt management plan and settled each debt over a 15-month period. He felt the debts were still hanging over him until they were finally paid off, and I asked him how it felt when he finally paid them off:

> "It wasn't really a celebration; I would say it was more relief… and… that this chapter of my life was now closed."

Darren now helps others with the same addiction and gave me important insights into the mindset of a gambler:

> "So if you're a gambler… you can be very secretive, almost creating another life. If you're gambling online, you're always on your phone. At home, you might intercept the mail. You're on edge a lot of the time and snap very easily. Sometimes you'll create an argument

just to get out of the house so you can just go and gamble. It just takes over your life."

In addition, there's the deceptive nature:

"Gamblers lie when they don't even need to lie. They're just so used to it, and it takes so much effort; one lie needs so many more. People go as far as changing their address so statements go elsewhere. They can just become a different person."

Vulnerable Communities

Working with Gamblers Anonymous, Darren sees a correlation between deprivation and gambling:

"Deprived areas and communities often turn to gambling as a means for survival."

One only has to consider a shortfall in money, a lack of shelter, food, or clothing, and, with the inability to buy loved ones gifts, an absence of the type of joy this would bring. Gambling simply amplifies the desperation as poor choices are made to try and rectify these difficult situations. Thus, one falls into a deeper life of *vikarma*, as previously described. With shortcuts to success and quick wins over long-term gain, gambling somehow becomes a necessity instead of a recreation.

The saintly, righteous, clean path of *karma* does not serve deprived communities well. Opportunities seem absent with the daily grind for survival. *Karma*, with its simple law of cause and effect, does not feed hungry bellies at the end of the day or provide warm coats for a fast-approaching winter. Low incomes cause a month to run out of money, and as the growing 'working poor' manifests in society, so does the desire for desperate money-making.

Poverty is a complex tangle, and in trying to undo one knot of impoverishment, a gambler ties another five, making the situation worse. But gambling is alluring, and the industry is very accessible, as Darren explained further:

> "The government put a cap on bets placed in spaces for gambling because they know gambling is a big problem in deprived areas. But online gambling has no cap, so it's almost irrelevant. You have a slogan now: 'when the fun stops, stop'… but it's the same as any addiction; as soon as you're addicted and hooked, you need that buzz throughout the day."

Betting companies would prefer people to bet online because there are very few overheads, and you can gamble twenty-four hours a day, which presents a further pernicious and insidious problem for the addiction.

Muffled by the Buzz

Darren also spoke of an inner voice, a voice that gets ignored by the thrill of the 'buzz' from gambling:

"This is the irrationality of it: everything under the banner of common sense tells me that I shouldn't be doing this. There's this voice saying, 'Right, I am not doing this today,' but a gambler always caves in. It's like your body *needs* it, and your mind *craves* it!"

Acknowledging that making it illegal would not help, Darren says that the industry would simply go underground:

"The fact is that gambling is a massive problem, and I don't see it getting any better. At least it's regulated and it's there for conversation. If people want to challenge things then they can because it's lawful as such. As soon as you ban it, you can't police it."

Dialogue and purpose

The path of a *yogī* and the path of a recovering gambler are not too dissimilar. The *yogī* wants to avoid getting intoxicated with the world's thrills and dive into the fulfilment within. The recovering gambler wants to draw their attention away from all avenues of gambling:

"You remove yourself from the opportunity to gamble by giving up control of your money; you remove access by blocking yourself from environments where gambling takes place."

Darren explains to recovering gamblers that there is software available to block gambling sites on devices and also advises self-exclusion from gambling shops and casinos. This is useful when a gambler, early on in recovery, might fall victim to a strong urge to gamble but is barred from the betting arena.

I am encouraged to know that Darren is available in these spaces, where he can enlighten people on the pervasive nature of gambling in our society. I see it at work all the time: light-hearted gambling is always around us – a simple sweep-stake for a football tournament, small bets on the Grand National, a little betting syndicate on the lottery or scratch cards while shopping. This conversation made me more conscious and Darren talked me through how he works with recovering gamblers in the beginning:

> "We just say, 'One day at a time, don't think too far ahead.' One day becomes two, then it turns to weeks and then months. The longer you stay off it, the stronger you get; the urge reduces over time. And the final thing is time… You have to fill your time, become busy, find a purpose."

Taking Account

Keeping a note of the last bet he ever took as a reference point for the years of his recovery, Darren speaks with wisdom looking back at this chapter of his life:

> "I've learnt at a great cost and given pain to the ones that I love."

Having been questioned, Darren couldn't say that he found joy in growing from the experience, as it involved the suffering of those he loved; it was soberingly honest:

"If I suffer and I come out a better person while no one is getting hurt, then happy days. But unfortunately, I hurt people in the process of becoming wise to it all. If I had just *talked* to my wife and got the help I ended up getting, then it would have been better. But then I ask, 'Did I need that incident in the van to actually stop?' Who knows."

Coming to terms with his addiction and recovery, Darren told me of his current mindset:

"I'm an intelligent guy. I know it's stupid, but if I keep asking why… why did I do it… well, it can just fry your brains. So I have to draw a line in the sand and say, 'Yep, I did it. I regret doing it, and I'm not going to do it again. And these are the reasons why.' If you always live in the past and keep worrying about the past, then you can just get stuck there. Sometimes, you've got to just put the past behind you and look to the future."

Clarity

Clearly free now, Darren would rather air the problem and learn from it, and let his experiences be a warning or a lesson:

"I see it for what it is now. Some people are not comfortable talking about it, but I'm under the impression that if you can talk about it and help people, then it's worth it. Dialogue is important."

Ancient Eastern philosophers often talked about a metaphysical world – the invisible world behind the physical world. This metaphysical world, in many ways, makes the physical world more real by bringing meaning and emotion to it. We can become aware of the subtle energy that lingers around the acts we perform, and gambling is no different. If you look closely enough, it is obvious that the energy that surrounds gambling is deceit.

While on a small level, a 'cheeky little bet' doesn't seem harmful, involvement in the game of chance has deception written all over it. The bigger the bet, the bigger the loss and the bigger the disappointment. The ensuing disgruntlement can bring us to the gateway of desperation. The unfortunate truth about gambling is that all gamblers are out to deceive each other, to win and not be deceived themselves, thus setting up a downward spiral into a quagmire that leaves them quintessentially stuck.

Add to this the knowledge that your wins and your joys involved the frustrations or even the pain of another person due to their losses. That's more metaphysical energy being absorbed. Is this the type of energy we want to absorb?

There is a famous story from Ancient Bhārat of the Emperor of Hastināpura, now the region of Meerut, Uttar Pradesh. His name was Yudhiṣṭhira, and he was challenged to a game of dice. The game was played in a public arena with many watching. He became so entrapped in the game that he lost his entire kingdom, and in his desperation, staked his own brothers and wife, only to lose them and become slaves. Ordinarily, Yudhiṣṭhira was a man of honour, truth, and justice, but the story shows the intoxicating and destructive nature of gambling. Taking claim of the lives of Yudhiṣṭhira and his family, his opponents dragged Yudhiṣṭhira's wife into the gambling hall and began to disrobe her.

Fundamentally, such highly speculative risk-taking that involves no due diligence is seen as a weakness of heart in Eastern scriptures. The particular weakness is the lack of willingness for honest work, for integrity in earnings, and honour in duty. The ancients of India, Bhārat, warn that gambling breaks down the virtues of truth, honesty, and Integrity – major pillars for a functioning society. Gambling breeds a culture of lying and deceit; therefore, we should become aware of this trait, for we all have a tendency to cheat, and it is how we deal with this propensity for cheating that will influence the outcome of our lives.

PART TWO

My Reflections on Recovery

Desperation

Darkness

Staring into the darkest region of the heart, I wonder where this hard road of life leads. I feel it leads to the depths of despair. The darker it gets, the more confusion and chaos seems to ensue. I regularly see people in extreme states of hopelessness who feel an urgency to commit desperate acts.

Lacking clarity, we saw Darren's (almost) last moments in his van, Dheep's attempt at taking her own life, Ezekiel's desire for money, and Robyn's search for revenge as examples of desperate moments.

Desperation can arrive through financial difficulties, relationship problems, health issues, job loss, or traumatic events. These stressors could combine and produce a sense of overwhelm, and in this anxious state of powerlessness, one could arrive at the gateway of mental health issues like depression.

Desperation causes a person to experience a range of intense and negative emotions, such as helplessness, fear, anger, and frustration, as well as feeling overwhelmed, stressed, and anxious. A desperate person may feel trapped and have a sense of urgency to produce a resolution despite having difficulty seeing a way out of their current situation.

Drastic measures to try and improve a situation may be taken but in impulsive ways. As desperation deepens, higher risk-taking may take course. Willing to engage in behaviours that are harmful to themselves or others, such as self-harm, violence, or suicide, it is essential to note that states of desperation lead to a person's judgement becoming impaired as their ability to make sound decisions becomes affected. Desperate states lead one to become more vulnerable to manipulation or exploitation by others, and so it becomes vitally important for people to seek help if they are in a state of desperation.

From Darkness to Light

These stories demonstrate how one can come out of hopelessness and despair.

1. Seeking help: Dheep reached out to a priest, Ezekiel spoke to a fellow inmate, and Darren joined a recovery group. Talking to a therapist, counsellor, or a trusted friend or family member can be an essential first step in dealing with feelings of desperation. They can provide support and guidance, and help identify the underlying causes of the feelings.

2. Developing a plan of action: Darren's strategies to help gambling addicts in recovery take themselves out of their toxic environment is an example of small, manageable steps that can be taken to improve the situation and help reduce feelings of helplessness and despair.

3. Finding ways to cope: All four of our heroes threw themselves into a purpose beyond themselves. Although I did not ask specifically what they do to manage stress, some common examples are conscious breathing, meditation, mindfulness, yoga, exercise, journalling, and managing one's time better. These are some established ways to help cope with feelings of desperation.

4. Building a support network: Ezekiel talked about creating a network and associating with people who are moving forward in life. It is self-evident that association is key, and the power of connecting with others who have gone through similar experiences can provide a sense of understanding and validation.

5. Seeking professional help: If a person is dealing with mental health conditions, such as depression or anxiety, that are contributing to feelings of desperation, then a professional in this field can be very beneficial. Robyn looked back at his 16-year-old self, suspicious of a depression that may have hit him, making me consider the need for access to professional care in every school, college and workplace moving forward.

6. Taking time for self-care: Dheep explained that she liked to walk in nature, Darren and Ezekiel enjoyed spending quality time with their children, and Robyn ensured he read regularly. Engaging in activities that bring joy and relaxation, such as reading, listening to

music, or spending time in nature, can help to reduce feelings of stress and anxiety.

Patience and the growth of optimism.

Transformation takes time, so patience and support are vital. Hope is the magnet that pulls one out of a state of desperation, and hope is the quintessential energy of optimism.

A hopeful person is optimistic and has a positive outlook on the future, believing that things will improve. They have a sense of agency and believe that their actions can improve their situation. Optimistic people have an understanding of resilience and are able to bounce back from adversity. They also have a sense of purpose and direction in life, making them less likely to be overwhelmed by negative emotions. Sensing this level of optimism at the end of each of my interviews filled me with hope, hope that people can recover, hope that things can improve, and hope in the human spirit.

The Renewal

Relief was the first overriding emotion I could sense drifting in when Dheep, Robyn, Darren, and Ezekiel's despair started to lift. Renewed with energy and motivation, they began to see a way out of their difficulties and take steps to improve their situation.

Fulfilled by their accomplishments, I could tell the transition must have taken time. I got a sense that it certainly was not a linear process, with ups and downs we may never get to hear about.

Wise to the fact that constant effort is needed to maintain sobriety, optimism, and hope, they all finished with a tone of gratitude that seemed to keep them anchored against arrogance or complacency, filling them with the sweet fruit found growing on the side of this hard road: humility.

Desperate hasty decisions are rarely wise
In the heat of the moment with no time to analyse
We make clouded judgements and decisions unclean
And trip over what is unseen
So let hope in with her glimmer
The shine and shimmer will delight
As awareness brings wisdom, and a move towards the light

The Futility and Utility of Audacity

Audacity: Two sides of a coin

Audacity allows us to face challenges which we otherwise would have avoided and I would certainly say that with all four of our heroes, audacity was at play. On one side, audacity makes us fearless enough to pursue an ideal; on the other it can also make us reckless enough to pursue chaos. Bearing witness to the events our heroes went through, we can learn from their mistakes. Seeing how our heroes tempered the boldness of their audacious spirit with caution, reasoning, and wisdom, we see stability, function, and beauty manifest in their lives.

The utility of audacity

Knowing Darren personally, I can say he had an audacious spirit throughout school, especially when comically speaking up against injustices that he saw. Dheep's move to New York was a bold step in her life. However, I sense that Ezekiel and Robyn's audacious spirit was met with judgement and disapproval, especially during their school years, begging the question around recognising a child's nature and how a daring spirit needs to be curbed, tempered, and even nurtured.

Audacity encompasses bold, daring, and even unconventional steps towards challenge or change, even if met with resistance. Sharpening a young person's audacious spirit can help them accomplish things that are normally considered impossible or unlikely for them. In the future, they may be able to challenge the status quo or be useful agents for transformation in society, tradition, or culture.

Assertiveness training that helps people make their points clearly, calmly, and concisely reduces the perception that someone is aggressive. Children need skills in this, especially as assertiveness and aggression are often categorised together. Thus helping someone become a leader without becoming a bully.

When we hit the sweet spot of audacity, positive outcomes such as innovation, progress, and personal growth occur. However, audacity is often misunderstood and overplayed.

When Audacity twists out of shape

When the fearlessness associated with audacity steps too far it, enters the realm of recklessness. Dheep fearlessly took drugs into her workplace, Darren lost thousands of pounds at a time, Ezekiel picked up firearms, and Robyn was unafraid of turning to violence on the streets. I myself have got into skirmishes and arguments by being overly-audacious in certain situations, only to regretfully pick up the pieces afterwards.

Recklessness grins broadly and lacks consideration for consequences. It disregards safety and well-being. Being reckless ensures people take unnecessary risks, ignore safety protocols, and disregard the advice of experts. It reduces empathy and inhibits the ability to perceive the needs of others. In this way, recklessness drags one down a treacherous path, and it is not always guaranteed that U-turns can be made.

Physiology of Wisdom.

Realising a deep need for change, our heroes found themselves a long distance from the threshold of recklessness and started to trudge back.

This realisation may actually be age-dependent, for the brain's prefrontal cortex is responsible for executive functions. These are the complex processes required for planning and deeper levels of decision-making. Examples include anticipating events in the environment, predicting the consequence of one's decisions, focusing one's attention, impulse control, and more.

The full development of the prefrontal cortex occurs around the age of 25, but can be stunted by trauma or addiction to substances. I can see why Robyn felt so strongly about not criminalising children and young adults who make unfortunate mistakes early in life.

Wise to his misgivings of a previous lifestyle, Ezekiel felt it necessary to teach the lesson of consequence to his daughter, informing her kindly about the danger of selling drugs.

Intentional use of the prefrontal cortex develops it. So it would serve society well if parents and educators consciously helped build these executive functions to help everyone on this path to wisdom.

The Rise of Integrity and Dignity

Does integrity mean having a clean life-long record of never making mistakes? Is that realistic? Or does it mean integrating with your weaknesses to learn from them and even make them a strength?

With our heroes, they patiently rebuilt their integrity day by day. Managing an audacious spirit meant they converted it into a working asset in their lives. Now they are not afraid to talk about their past, for their journey gives hope to future souls with similar tendencies.

A year later, touching base with each of our heroes, I saw how dignity had arisen in each of their lives. They do not shy away from being honest – honest about the weakness of the human condition, what it takes to admit there is a problem, and how an earnest attempt at changing one's life is the only way to make a turnaround.

Audacity.
Fiery, bold and bright
The strength to face our fears and fight
But it might overflow
Bring recklessness and show
Doorways to dark places unknown
So carry audacity in the heart
But don't depart
From Wisdom
And the voice of reason

Two Roads, One Goal: Virtue, Vice and Wisdom

The premise upon which this whole book sits is that while virtue leads to wisdom, so too does the road of vice. Virtue, vice, and wisdom are closely related concepts. Virtue refers to the moral excellence and righteousness of an individual, while vice refers to the opposite: immoral behaviour. In Sanskrit, virtue is known as being attractive (*ākarṣaka*) while vice is seen as repulsive (*vibhatsa*). Therefore virtue and vice are two sides of a coin. Wisdom (*viveka*) is be the end goal and is an understanding of how the pendulum swings between the two.

Wisdom is the ability to make sound judgements, decisions that are in line with one's values and beliefs. Together, these three concepts guide individuals so their choices lead to a fulfilling and meaningful life.

Enhanced emotional intelligence, better decision-making capabilities, improved problem-solving, greater well-being, enhanced resilience, and improved communication all come from the presence of wisdom. Developed by a combination of life experience, reflection, and self-awareness, wisdom proves to be the essence of understanding, education, and learning.

Understanding comes from empathy while exposure to diverse experiences and cultures makes us wise. We must, therefore, challenge ourselves to converse with people from all walks of life and, remaining curious, open both our hearts and minds.

The Misconception

There is often a misconception that it is only virtue that leads us to wisdom, but on the contrary, it is the battle with vice and the realization of how powerful it is that leads us to appreciate virtue and truly develop wisdom. If virtue were a mountain and reaching the top were deemed virtuous, then the shadow that the mountain casts would represent vice. Amidst the shadows would lurk the vicious habits that sabotage us. Then what would be wisdom? Well, wisdom would be the light itself, for *viveka* (wisdom) means illumination.

Let us look at an example. Generosity versus miserliness. Generosity is a virtue and people who make charitable contributions are celebrated and get placed on this proverbial mountain. Miserly people, on the other hand, are placed in the darkness of the shadows. However, wisdom will see many other things. Wisdom may see that charitable people give because they have the capacity to give and have developed an abundance mindset. Wisdom would also caution us and say that a charitable person may become too egotistical and proud at times. Wisdom would caution us to not judge the miser too soon, for they might have come from a needy, traumatic background with scarcity, and their hoarding is their way of seeking security. Wisdom would say that a miser may eventually see the bitterness of their ways and open up to generosity. Wisdom would also say a generous person could become bitter and stop giving, or see how their giving nature becomes tiresome and a detriment to themselves, and thus draw a boundary around their giving nature. Therefore, it is not the applause of reaching the mountain that is the goal; it is bathing in the light of wisdom.

In reality, there are two paths to wisdom: the bright and glorious path of virtue, and the dark and vicious path of vice. Individuals are not confined to one path or another; they ebb and flow between the two, following either path at different times in their lives.

The path of virtue is more desirable as it appears more sanitary, associated with positive behaviours like honesty, compassion, and responsibility but what value do they have if not pipped against cheating, exploitation and disregard? We are often repelled by those on the unsavoury road of vice, as it is associated with negative behaviours such as lying, selfishness, and irresponsibility. However, seeing reality is seeing that, on both roads, we can become ensnared.

Two Paths, Two Prisons

Virtue brings glory, and vice brings pain. Vice is an obvious prison, but virtue can also become a prison – an ethereal prison of the ego.

Living by virtue can contribute to building character, promoting ethical decision-making, and encouraging empathy. However, we may trip up on some of virtue's pitfalls.

Virtue brings glory, and a glorious life might bring parasites like self-righteousness and arrogance. Rigidity to a virtue makes a person dogmatic, and their inability to bend or make allowances can lead them to confusion. A dogmatic person cannot always see the negative results of their actions and often ignores the context or culture they are in. Therefore, virtue can have trappings and even lead to vice eventually.

Vice, on the other hand, certainly has many negative effects. Self-destructive behaviours, causing harm to others, problems with finance and achieving goals, negative impact on reputation and integrity, as well as a decrease in well-being, are all effects of vice. This prison of the difficult road is obvious, but it be can worked through if we do not lose one thing: hope.

Hope (*āśā*) seems to be one of the 'virtue of virtues' and is up there with compassion (*dayā*). Without the tiny beam of light that is hope, there is only darkness.

Several strategies can be used to work through vice. If one can identify their vice, set clear goals, create a plan, and seek support, then they can begin to change their behaviour. They certainly may have to do some deep work, like Ezekiel King in his prison cell, addressing the underlying issues with the practice of self-compassion.

Who would appreciate the view from the top of this virtue mountain? The person who was placed there, or the one who scaled its heights through the treacherous shadows? There is much to be celebrated when a person in recovery reaches milestones and gains a deeper state of wisdom, especially when it is more insightful than the person who has only walked the virtuous path.

In summary then, the benefits of virtue are apparent while the trappings are subtle. When it comes to vice, the downfalls are obvious, but the benefits are subtle. The realised experiences of the heart and mind are incredibly valuable and difficult to break.

Breaking Free

Working through vice involves understanding our own weaknesses and flaws which leads to personal growth. Recognising and acknowledging one's own vices is a sign of maturity and allows us to take steps to overcome them. A richer life is potentially there, just around the corner.

Additionally, working through vice can also help us build resilience and inner strength as we learn to navigate and overcome difficult challenges and obstacles.

Working through vice, we can also develop empathy and understanding towards others. Dheep set up a consultancy to help professionals with similar problems as herself, Darren became an integral part of his local Gambling Anonymous group, and both Robyn and Ezekiel regularly speak to teenagers and young adults to share their experiences and wisdom to help others make better choices in life. Gaining a deeper understanding of the human condition through overcoming vice seems to fill one with compassion. There appears to be an incredible ability to connect and relate to others, mainly due to earnest and sincere openness – fantastic ingredients for trust and rapport.

With the wisdom gained from conquering vice, an individual can gain a deeper understanding of the world and their place in it. Greater insights create a holistic perspective and a shared reality which leads to better decision-making and fulfilling life choices.

The Gifts of Vice

The dark road of vice is certainly littered with negativity and pain, but it is also glittered with gifts like gratitude and humility, which create depth in one's life. Building resilience and inner strength helps navigate and overcome difficult challenges that will inevitably appear further down the road.

In the darkness, we trip on the litter,
Only to pick ourselves up and see what glitters
Gratitude, humility and acceptance
…of what was simply meant to be.

Inner Voice

Talking to My Self

Self-talk that occurs within one's mind refers to the inner voice. This inner dialogue can be either positive or negative and influences our thoughts, emotions, and actions.

Shaped by our beliefs, values, and past experiences, our inner voice is further influenced by media, social norms, and the opinions of others. It can be a source of self-motivation, self-doubt, encouragement, or negative self-talk. Remarkably, all four of our heroes mentioned an inner voice of reason that they seemed to either dismiss or disregard which would lead to self-sabotage.

Sometimes, our inner voice can be overly critical or negative, bringing with it feelings of low self-esteem and self-doubt. Challenging negative thoughts is therefore important. Ezekiel looked at his life objectively, Robyn challenged the value of revenge and violence when he saw the blood-stained floor, Darren safeguarded himself against temptation, and Dheep had a mystical experience shedding layers of a false and impermanent identity. An inner voice guided all of this.

Several factors can make someone susceptible to the negative inner voice. These include past experiences such as trauma or abuse, low self-esteem, social-cultural influences, mental health issues, or a lack of self-awareness.

Susceptibility is not a permanent state and can be changed with practice, self-reflection, self-awareness, and seeking help if necessary.

Developing a positive and supportive inner dialogue is essential work. It improves one's self-confidence and resilience. Wisdom speaks from within kindly, mindfully, equipoised, and balanced to produce self-compassion, and guide us towards thriving and fulfilment.

Intuition

Senses that navigate the physical world exist, such as seeing and hearing. However, there are senses within us that are subtle – invisible senses that can perceive the imperceptible. Feeling or sensing something to be true or right without any logical reasoning can be considered instinctual or a 'gut feeling.' It is like an inner voice that speaks to you without using words, often associated with a sense of knowing or understanding. It becomes difficult to explain or put into words; in Sanskrit, this inconceivable nature of the inner voice is known as *acintya*. Dheep experienced this voice dramatically, and she trusted it. The voice of intuition, often associated with creativity, decision-making, and problem-solving, when combined with positivity and logic, can develop an internal sense of intuition that serves us and humanity as well.

Two Voices

Christian imagery of a small devilish creature sitting on one shoulder arguing with an angel that sits on the other comes to mind. There is also the Native American metaphor of two dogs living within us: one good and one bad. This highlights the timeless nature of this struggle within the human experience and the need to be aware of the competing voices in our psyche. The advice from wise Native Americans goes further, stating that the dog we feed more becomes stronger and louder, inferring that it is us and our positive or negative mindset that guides the strength and stance of our internal voice.

A good inner voice would be wise and supportive. Offering guidance, encouragement, and constructive criticism to help us make good decisions to reach our goals. Good inner voices remind us of our strengths and capabilities, helping us stay focused and motivated. This cheerful inner voice can be a constructive force in our lives, helping us navigate the challenges and obstacles that come our way.

A bad inner voice is harsh. Like a constantly displeased drill sergeant who is judgemental, demanding, and relentlessly dissatisfied. Finding fault in everything we do makes us feel like we are not good enough. Intimidating and discouraging, the negative inner voice makes us doubt our abilities, making us feel like giving up. This pessimistic inner voice thus becomes an opposing force in our lives, holding us back and making it difficult to achieve our goals.

I do not believe this negative voice needs to be dispelled completely, for that would breed pathological positivity. Instead, I believe it can evolve into a healthy, pragmatic, and sceptical voice that is humorously cynical and rationally doubtful—a balanced voice of reason.

Sabotage of the Self

Self-sabotage is the process of unconsciously undermining our own goals, aspirations, or interests. Manifesting in various ways, it can be difficult to identify self-sabotage, but common examples are procrastination, self-doubt, self-medication, self-isolation, deliberately handicapping oneself, and perfectionism.

Self-defeating and hyper-critical inner voices are harmful to our mental and emotional well-being. Self-deprecating thoughts can lead to low self-esteem, depression, and anxiety, while the inner voice that is excessively worried and anxious leads to a state of panic. Panic is harmful in a number of ways, especially when it leads to the avoidance of important situations like facing a bill or having that important conversation with an angry neighbour. Panic might also cause us to partake in activities that limit our ability to function or thrive on a day-to-day basis like binge-watching a television series, using intoxicants, or eating in excess. An anxious person becomes desperate, and a desperate person is vulnerable.

All of this centres on negative self-talk, driven mainly by fear. Fear of failure, rejection, change, or even the fear of success often ends up preventing us from fulfilling our potential.

Recognising self-sabotaging behaviours is the first step in changing them, making it essential to understand the underlying thoughts and feelings that sabotage rests upon. Developing healthy coping mechanisms, positive self-talk, setting realistic goals, and seeking support from others are some ways we can overcome self-sabotaging patterns.

All four of our heroes made this change and stopped sabotaging themselves, retuning their inner frequencies to listen to the positive voice within, which had been muffled or gagged by emotion or circumstance.

Voice of Delusion

Deeper into negativity is the voice of delusion, which leads to irrational thoughts, beliefs, and behaviours that are not based on reality, bringing terrible potential for harm to an individual's mental and/or physical health.

I work with teenagers and young adults to help them understand reality more. It's a beginner's level of philosophical discussion that defines the reality of themselves in an engaging way. We talk about four layers of ourselves going from most external to internal. Firstly there is the physical, then the physiological, the subtle psychological and, finally, the philosophical. Understanding all four of these means understanding the self.

The philosophical self is the deepest and helps define our reality. It is a filter through which we watch the world and judge our situation. In this regard, a person would be served well if they understood axiomatic truths, and so I have age-appropriate conversations to help develop this understanding. I feel it's important because it can be understood from a very young age and forms the basis of self-knowledge. Knowledge of the self becomes the blueprint and foundation for real knowledge. Axiomatic truths, called *tattva* in Sanskrit are fundamental, indivisible aspects of reality that are used to comprehend life. As one understands *tattva*, one journeys out of delusion. For *tattva* literally means 'that which exists.'

Conversing in terms of the autonomous multifaceted soul, called the *ātman*, and the physical world of procreation called *prakṛti*, my students begin a journey of self-actualisation, gaining perspective as we complete self-exploratory exercises from the world of coaching. By looking at how these two fundamental aspects of reality interact via time (*kāla*) and the law of cause and consequence known as *karma*, these students start to develop hindsight, foresight, and insight, wisdom of their own which will serve them for the rest of their lives.

Fear is a rickety bridge above the abyss of meaninglessness and delusion, while solid ground is what forms with a healthy definition of reality. The more we understand reality, the more the abyss shrinks. Clarity and a healthy outlook of reality feed the voice of security and confidence.

Frequency Retune

Ultimately, listening to both the pros and cons of a situation leads to making a balanced decision, and so developing an intuitive voice of wisdom over both the positive and negative voices is a process that requires time and effort. There are strategies that can help, such as mindfulness, reflection, listening to our body, trusting ourselves, and seeking help from professionals, experts, or wise well-wishers. Re-tuning our receptors to the frequency of wisdom means we challenge negativity but also learn from it or even laugh at it. Positivity can be pathological if we are overly optimistic, but practising positive self-talk is necessary.

The negative inner voice cannot be silenced forever; it will always be there. However, with practice, we can learn to recognise it, challenge it, appease it, and even learn from it. Eventually, the inner voice of intuition emerges, balancing emotion and logic, the positive and negative, and draws out the rational from the absurd.

Future

Like Ezekiel and Robyn, I strongly hope that future generations are blessed with an education system that evolves them internally through self-reflection and self-awareness. For me, this would mean developing the philosophical self as early as possible to strengthen one's voice of intuition.

A person who is more in tune with their intuitive voice is likely to have had better life experiences, has practised some degree of mindfulness, has good social support, and matures as they age. Genetics certainly also plays a part in naturally having a healthy intuition.

My students who are mindful, reflective, open to feedback, unafraid of trying new things, practice self-compassion, are curious and ask for help when required, seem to develop their self-awareness at a greater rate. This, in turn, makes them wiser. As a reminder to us all, I will repeat that wisdom—symbolically represented by light—helps develop clarity and fulfilment.

My advice to my students is always to have a good network, keep good counsel, and be open to challenges, remembering that self-awareness is a lifelong journey that takes time and practice.

When negativity grips my mind
And self-doubt starts to bind
I breathe…
And build a bridge across the sea
From chaos and confusion…
to clarity.

Concluding Thoughts

In conclusion, the journeys of Dheep, Robyn, Ezekiel, and Darren serve as examples of resilience, determination, and the power of transformation. Despite seemingly insurmountable challenges, they persevered and turned their lives around to find purpose, joy, and fulfilment.

I am intrigued by the common elements in all of these stories—the inner voice, audacity, and desperation—and hope we can find meaning in these patterns.

Through their trials and tribulations, these stories offer hope to those who may feel hopeless and encouragement to those feeling downtrodden by their circumstances. They prove that no matter how far one may fall, it is never too late to get back up, make a change, and build a better life. These individuals serve as shining examples of the human spirit's capacity to overcome adversity, and they will surely continue to inspire and encourage others for years to come.

Dheep wrote a book of memoirs about her addiction and awakening called *A New York Kind of Love*, and Robyn authored a series of books, starting with *Prisoner to the Streets* and became a coach, helping youth and young adults make better life choices. Ezekiel wrote a crime novel called *From Innocence to Arrogance*, and Darren regularly facilitates his local Gambling Anonymous recovery group, helping people recover from their gambling addiction and clear their debts to renew their lives.

While writing this book, other than telling these four stories for reasons I've already shared, I hope to have sparked an interest in the pursuit of wisdom within you and an appreciation for the teleological nature of Sanskrit, the ancient language from the tradition I belong to. The teleological nature of Sanskrit means that it has, coded within it, an ability to unlock deep lessons about life like duty, values, character, virtue, vice, wisdom, and much more.

Doing these interviews, I have learnt about the trappings of virtue and the gifts of vice. It has made me less judgemental about people trapped by their patterns of behaviour or the nature of their circumstances.

I invite you to reflect further on the themes of desperation, audacity, the inner voice, and how we ensnare ourselves. This reflection can bring understanding into your own life and encourage dialogue with those around you to increase connection and empathy.

Curious to know, more I am already conducting further interviews to follow up on this book. Looking at adolescence, the systems of education, sex addiction, grief, and the impact of suicide on those left behind as well as the play of power and exploitation. I hope to spread further insights and inspire change where it is needed.

This life is full of pitfalls but if you fall into a pit, I want you to feel like there is a way of getting out, that there is hope. These four stories prove that. The human spirit is beautiful, pure consciousness striving for bliss, eternality, and knowledge resolute. Why? Because we are made of these things.

Finally, the winding roads to wisdom are only the beginning. Wisdom is the foundation for a secure and functioning life. There is something beyond wisdom, and that is love. Wisdom is the essence while love is the quintessence. If wisdom were the North Pole, then Love would be the North Star, a heavenly body guiding us beyond the light of wisdom.

> *Beyond a life of security and function,*
> *There is a life of Beauty and Love.*
> *A vibrant and deeper spectrum…*
> *Of light beyond the light.*